Simply *in* Season
Leader's Study Guide

Rachel Miller Moreland

D1563560

Herald Press
Scottdale, Pennsylvania
Waterloo, Ontario

Library of Congress Cataloging-in-Publication Data

Miller-Moreland, Rachel.
    Simply in season study guide : a six-session leader's guide / Rachel
Miller Moreland.
      p. cm.
    ISBN 0-8361-9342-3 (pbk. : alk. paper)
    1. Food in the Bible—Study and teaching. 2. Food—Religious
aspects—Christianity—Study and teaching. 3. Stewardship, Christian—Study
and teaching. I. Lind, Mary Beth. Simply in season. II. Title.
    BS680.F6M55 2006
    268'.434--dc22

                                    2006030495

Rachel Miller Moreland was a writer in the Communications Department of
Mennonite Central Committee, and helped with the cookbook *Simply in Season*. She
currently lives in western Ohio.

Acknowledgments: Thanks to Cathleen Hockman-Wert for her input and to the
Sunday school classes who tested an early version of the study guide: Jubilee
Mennonite Church (Bellefontaine, Ohio), East Petersburg Mennonite Church (East
Petersburg, Pa.), and a group of Mennonite young adults in Washington, D.C.

To order or request information, please call
1-800-759-4447 (individuals); 1-800-245-7894 (trade).
www.heraldpress.com

Preface

Welcome to a journey toward joy-filled, meaningful eating. Based on themes in the *Simply in Season* cookbook, this study guide is designed to lead adult or intergenerational Sunday school classes or small groups on a path to connecting food and faith, with an emphasis on the value of eating local, seasonal food.

There are six core sessions and seven optional sessions. A unique feature of this material is that while the leader uses this study guide, the "textbook" for each participant is actually the cookbook.

SPREADING THE WORD

If you are trying to raise interest and attract participants to a Sunday school or congregation-based small group to study this material, try getting creative. Adapt this two-person drama format for announcements during a church service:

"Maria" is eating an apple. "Mike" walks by.

Mike: Hey, Maria, what'cha doin'?

Maria: Enjoying this tasty apple from the local orchard.

Mike: Really? Looks to me like you're helping to care for God's creation (care for your local community, conserve oil and water, create a more just world, etc.). (Turning to the congregation) If you want to learn more about how your eating choices can reflect your faith, come to ... (give class details).

Do a series of announcements, focusing on the various themes (creation, time, money, health). Substitute other food items for the apple. You can couple this with snacks provided during a fellowship time. For example, bring a basket of the apples "Maria" is eating. You may want to include a small sign by the snack with a question like, "Can eating these apples help you live out your faith?" and the details of the class.

How to Guide

First, make sure each participant has a *Simply in Season* cookbook. This is their "textbook."

The sessions in this guide are designed for a typical hour-long Sunday school class; adapt them to your needs. There are six core sessions. Seven additional optional sessions (on pages 42-61) can be used to explore a theme from a core session more deeply.

Page numbers that are noted throughout the sessions refer to the *Simply in Season* cookbook.

CORE SESSIONS INCLUDE:

- Key ideas

- Materials needed

- Bible reflection (expanding on the verses that begin each chapter of the *Simply in Season* cookbook)

- Review and sharing time, activities, readings from the *Simply in Season* cookbook and discussion questions (in bold)

- Preview/Review handout that participants can take home to help guide their reflection and preparation for the next core session (Printer-friendly versions are available to download online at simplyinseason.org.)

You may choose to open with the Bible reflection, or incorporate that material into another part of the session. You may wish to have all the readings read aloud, or choose those that seem most appropriate. Large groups may want to break into smaller groups for some discussions. If time allows, invite relevant guest speakers for each session.

OPTIONAL SESSIONS INCLUDE:

Each optional session includes a description, preparation needed, and suggested session order. Components of the optional sessions are more varied, since these sessions range from watching and discussing a video to hosting a panel of local farmers. Some of the optional sessions are designed to immediately follow a core session by expanding on its themes; see the optional sessions section for suggested order.

Even if your group is using only the core sessions, leaders will benefit by looking over the related optional sessions for information, resources, and ideas.

INCORPORATING FOOD

What's a class on the value of local, seasonal food if it doesn't include some local, seasonal food? To help tie participants' experience to their own area and season, we suggest you either use local food to make a seasonal recipe from *Simply in Season* every week, or bring in a locally purchased item (in-season fruit, for example). This will require some creativity during the winter months. Ideally, this responsibility will be shared by all participants. Tell the story of the food as it's being served and note whether you made any substitutions. Participants can write notes on particular recipes in their copies of the cookbook.

INVESTIGATING LOCAL RESOURCES

An important role for leaders is seeking local resources: farmers' markets, community supported farms, and people involved in various aspects of farming and food production. Web sites that may be helpful in this search are listed in the Resources section at the end of this guide.

HELPING SHARE IDEAS

Participants will also do their own investigating of local resources, and the Preview/Review handouts invite participants to brainstorm ideas on various topics. Participants will also be encouraged to write their own prayers based on the topics in each session. Leaders should think about ways to share these ideas. Perhaps an e-mail listserve would suit your group best. Or hang up large pieces of paper in your meeting place and have participants write their ideas there. Prayers could be hung on a bulletin board and decorated with artwork if desired. You may also want to put together a booklet (or a final e-mail message) that compiles all these resources, ideas, and prayers.

OUTSIDE THE "CLASSROOM"

You may want to organize trips for your group or interested participants outside of your regular meeting time, perhaps to tour a local farm or orchard, or to visit a farmers' market.

SESSION 1
Food Stories

KEY IDEAS

· All food has a story. It comes to us through a "food (production) chain" of people and places—a chain that is growing increasingly long.

· Eating is a spiritual act, because our food choices affect everyone in this chain: God's children and God's creation.

· Shortening our chain—by choosing local, seasonal food—introduces joyful rhythms into our everyday lives, and is a way to address world problems that seem over-whelming.

MATERIALS NEEDED

- *Simply in Season* cookbook for each participant (as for all sessions)
- Paper and pencil for each participant
- Three tomatoes—one from a supermarket, two locally grown—or something to represent them, perhaps red balls (for Three Tomatoes' Stories activity)
- Three large pieces of paper (or a whiteboard) and thick markers
- Copies of Review/Preview handout found at end of this session (Printer-friendly versions are available to download online at simplyinseason.org.)

BIBLE REFLECTION

"They shall all sit under their own vines and their own fig trees, and they shall live in peace and unafraid." (Micah 4:4)

The prophet Micah lived at a time of extreme social and political upheaval. The Hebrew kingdoms, Judah and Israel, faced idolatry and injustice within and constant threats of violence without, particularly from the Assyrian empire, which succeeded in conquering Israel in 722-721 BC. In the passage that begins in Micah 4, the prophet describes a longed-for future in which God's peace and security reign. His description of God's people enjoying "their own vines and their own fig trees" is a proverbial picture of contentment also employed by other biblical authors to describe an idyllic past or future (see 1 Kings 4:25 and Zechariah 3:10).

Why was this image equated with peace? Having access to one's own source of food and drink was, as it is today, a great source of security. Yet the image of every person with a vine or fig tree is not one solely of self-reliance. Vineyards and trees, more than other crops, require years and even decades to reach their full potential. Wars, which destroy homes and scatter families, and the threat of war make such long-term investments in a piece of land impossible. In addition, in order for everyone to have the ability to grow food, a community must share its resources—water, suitable soil, etc.—equitably. As it is today, an ideal food system is linked both symbolically and literally to much larger international and local relationships.

1.

INTRODUCTION: Welcome participants to the class/small group. Explain that they—and you—are about to embark on a journey. While participants will be asked to examine some of their own assumptions and actions, it's important to remember that the goal of this journey is joy, not guilt. Give a brief overview of how the class will be structured and the expectations for study and reflection outside of class. Take a few moments to acquaint participants with the cookbook, pointing out the fruit and vegetable guide, resource list, index to writings, and recipe index. Explain that recipes are arranged by season, and each chapter's writings focus on one theme (for example, the Spring chapter focuses on the environment). If you've brought food made with locally grown items, pass it around now.

2.

Have you ever thought about the acts of choosing food and eating as religious or spiritual acts? In what sense? An idea that is likely to come up is that of our bodies as God's temple and our responsibility to care for individual health/weight. Encourage participants to also think beyond the individual level to how our choices affect our communities and the larger world.

3.

READINGS

"Increasing insecurity about food security" (p. 286)
"Shortening the food chain" (p. 187)
Use these readings to intoduce the idea of the food production chain.

4.

ACTIVITY: THREE TOMATOES' STORIES

This activity presents three possible food production chain scenarios for a tomato. First read the scenario, and then ask participants to list all the people who might be involved in the chain. For each person listed, have a participant stand at the front of the room to become a member of the chain.

After the chain of people is formed, ask the final member, the consumer, if he or she would be able to answer these questions: When was this tomato picked? How were the people who picked it treated? What kind of fertilizer was used? What percentage of the cost will the farmer and farm workers receive? The longer the food chain, the less we can know about our food. Note that while a long food chain may seemingly provide more jobs, these jobs are often low-paying (three in five farm worker households, for example, live below the poverty line) and less money is invested back in the local community.

If possible, bring in actual tomatoes—one from a supermarket, two locally grown—to pass down the chains. Supermarket tomatoes will stand up much better to rough handling. Then give participants a taste of the tomatoes.

Scenario 1: Tomato grown by a large agribusiness, shipped 1,400 miles (the average for a piece of produce) and purchased at a supermarket. Chain members could include:
• People who provide the grower with seeds, fertilizer, pesticides
• Owners of the agribusiness
• Migrant workers who pick the tomato
• Truck driver who transports the tomato
• Supermarket owner and workers
• Consumer

Scenario 2: Tomato purchased at local farmers' market. Chain members could include:
• People who provide seeds, fertilizer, pesticides (if applicable)
• Grower
• Stand worker
• Consumer

Scenario 3: Homegrown tomato, grown without chemicals from saved seeds. Chain member is:
• Grower / consumer

5.
What foods did you eat yesterday? You may allow time for participants to jot this down on paper. Do you know the story behind any of them? Were any of the ingredients grown near your home? Are they currently in season near your home? What is your connection to those who grew the food, picked it, prepared it?

6.
BRAINSTORMING: The following questions are designed to get participants thinking about topics covered in future sessions. For time reasons, treat this portion of the discussion as a brainstorming session rather than as a time for in-depth analysis. As participants respond, jot their answers on three large pieces of paper that you can hang up and

refer to in sessions to come. Label the lists "Factors/Values," "World Problems," and "Micah 4:4."

What factors play into your decisions about which foods to buy? It's important to acknowledge the very real obstacles of limited time, money, and knowledge. Encourage participants to also frame this response in a positive way, in terms of values we put into practice— that is, we want our food choices to reflect our values of being good stewards of our time, money, health, environment, etc.

List the world problems that seem the most overwhelming. These will likely include poverty, national security, and environmental damage. Explain that future sessions will explore how eating local, seasonal food can help address some of these problems.

How close are we to Micah's description of a world in which God's love and justice rule and we are all well fed, both physically and spiritually? What are the characteristics of such a world?

7.
CLOSING: If you've brought food, share its story with the class. Pass out the Review/Preview handouts (next page) and look over them. Point out the prayer component and note that prayer and food have always been connected, from blessings before meals to "Give us this day our daily bread" requests for God's provision. In this tradition, there are prayers in every chapter of the *Simply in Season* cookbook. You as the leader may want to do the "homework" a week ahead of time and show your own prayers as an example. Conclude with prayer—perhaps "A blessing of hands" (p. 333).

REVIEW SESSION 1
Food Stories

KEY IDEAS

• All food has a story. It comes to us through a "food (production) chain" of people and places—a chain that is growing increasingly long.

• Eating is a spiritual act, because our food choices affect everyone in this chain: God's children and God's creation.

• Shortening our chain—by choosing local, seasonal food—introduces joyful rhythms into our everyday lives, and is a way to address world problems that seem overwhelming.

PRAYER

Think of the people who form the chain that produce your food. Pray for them. Write out a prayer of blessing and gratitude for your food chain members.

INVITATIONS TO ACTION

• At the grocery store where you usually shop, see what information is available about where the produce has been grown. How about the meat, milk, and eggs? Is any of it local?

• Get local: Visit a local farmers' market, if you have one, and learn what's in season now. If your nearest market is not currently in operation, seek out information about when it will open and what kinds of foods it generally sells.

• Explore one of the Invitations to Action from the All Seasons chapter (p. 334).

PREVIEW SESSION 2
Creation

Skim the *Simply in Season* Spring chapter, which focuses on creation care.

Reflect on this scripture: "Yahweh, what variety you have created arranging everything so wisely: Earth is completely full of things you have made" (Psalms 104:24). How have you found joy in God's creation?

SESSION 2
Creation

KEY IDEAS

Environmental issues are not separate from overall human concerns. The health of the air, soil, water, and wildlife are directly related to our own health, and to that of our children and grandchildren.

Modern agribusiness is focused on producing large quantities at low financial cost.

"Sustainable agriculture" is focused on creating a system that can go on indefinitely. It must be economically viable, but it also must care for the land and provide a good quality of life for all concerned.

MATERIALS NEEDED

- Large piece of paper or whiteboard and marker
- Copies of Review/Preview handout found at end of this session (Printer-friendly versions are available to download online at simplyinseason.org.)

BIBLE REFLECTION

"Yahweh, what variety you have created arranging everything so wisely: Earth is completely full of things you have made." (Psalms 104:24)

Psalm 104 is a hymn of praise to God the Creator. The author extols the wonders of springs and rain, trees and grass, livestock and wild animals. Human labor is mentioned (in verse 23), but God is portrayed as the ultimate source of growth and decay, life and death. This attitude of awe toward the Creator runs throughout the Bible—see, for example, Job 38 and 39, in which God's power is beautifully equated with his intimate knowledge of and care for his creation. Inherent in this outlook is a sense of humans' vulnerability and need to rely on God in the face of powerful, mysterious forces (Psalm 104:29-30).

Today, with the advent of modern science and humans' perception of greater control over their environment, much of this awe for creation and its Creator has been lost. Standing in a supermarket surrounded by abundance, it's hard to feel anything but secure. Yet two pillars of our current conventional food system—large-scale irrigation, and reliance on fossil fuel at nearly every stage of production and transportation—leave us extremely vulnerable, both to human-made disruption and to the natural exhaustion of nonrenewable resources. Regaining a biblical sense of our own dependence on God and our connectedness to God's creation may be a first step toward rethinking this system.

1.

REVIEW: Allow time to share participants' prayers and responses to invitations to action. If you are posting input, hang up participants' prayers and begin making a list of local resources. (Alternately, e-mail these all to one person who will distribute them via e-mail.)

2.

READINGS

Psalms 104 (or selected verses)

"Today the air feels pregnant with spring" (p. 32)

Psalms 104 thanks God for the variety of creation, and this *Simply in Season* piece celebrates finding joy in creation. **How have you found joy in God's creation? Is there a piece of land (your garden or backyard, a park, your CSA farm) to which you currently feel connected?**

3.

How are environmental issues connected to quality of life for humans? How is caring for creation part of the Christian mission to care for humans, God's children? If your group already feels strongly that Christians are called to be responsible stewards of creation, spend minimal time on this question. However, if participants associate environmental issues only with New Age thinking or extremist groups, explore it more in depth. Point out that caring for the earth is about much more than, say, saving obscure species of animals: The big picture means preserving the resources (water, air, soil) without which we humans cannot survive.

4.

Have you personally observed or heard of environmental damage from agriculture in your area? If so, how has it affected the community?

5.

Relatively recent changes in how crops are grown and animals are raised help us feed more people, more cheaply than ever before. What are the tradeoffs involved in this system?

6.

ACTIVITY: EATING OIL

It has been said that modern agriculture is the process of turning petroleum into food. In the United States, agriculture accounts directly for 17 percent of the country's total fossil fuel consumption. Where does all this fossil fuel go as it changes into food?

Ask class members to list the steps in agricultural production that use fossil fuel. The top five are as follows:

31 percent—fertilizer (mostly through the natural gas-powered creation of inorganic nitrogen fertilizer)
19 percent—operation of field machinery
16 percent—transportation (not including transportation to stores)
13 percent—irrigation
8 percent—raising livestock (not including livestock feed)

And that's only a fraction of the total energy consumption that goes into our food. Ask the class to list other steps, such as packaging (think plastic), processing, transportation to retail outlets, and household storage and cooking. These additional steps consume even more energy than growing the food in the first place.

Supplies of fossil fuels are limited, and much violence around the world is linked to securing them. Do we have a responsibility to reduce the amount of oil in our food?

(It's important to note that agriculture's toll on the environment is nothing new. Throughout history, communities and even entire societies have become unsustainable because they exhausted their soil, polluted their water, or otherwise abused finite resources. But because our current system is being carried out on such a large scale, its potential for damage—to the earth and thus to humans' quality of life—is also huge. So how do we respond?

Sources: www.sustainabletable.org; "Eating Fossil Fuel," by Dale Allen Pfeiffer, available at www.fromthewilderness.com; "The Oil in Your Oatmeal," by Chad Heeter, San Francisco Chronicle, *March 26, 2006, www.sfgate.com)*

7.
ACTIVITY: IT'S HOPELESS!
This drama is intended to be humorous. Its success depends on Sally's character being completely over the top. Feel free to shout, point, and jump up and down.

Sally (wild-eyed activist type): Hi, Sam, what are you up to?

Sam (regular guy): Enjoying a hamburger.

Sally: Don't you mean destroying the earth? Polluting the soil, air, and water? Making the planet uninhabitable for our children and grandchildren?

Sam: Uhhh …

Sally: The wheat for that bun was probably grown in a huge field owned by a corporation, with petroleum-based fertilizers and gas-guzzling equipment. Don't you know that monoculture erodes soil quality and requires more pesticides? Or that run-off from fertilizer contaminates water supplies? Or that irrigation on a large scale usually wastes an unacceptable amount of our precious, precious water?

Sam: Uhhh …

Sally: And the meat! The cattle for that beef were probably raised in a feedlot. Do you know what that does to local air quality? The flies, and the smell? Not to mention all the antibiotics and growth hormones stuffed into those poor cows—and then into you?

Sam: Uhhh …

Sally: And then think of all the fossil fuels that go into harvesting, storing and transporting all those parts of your sandwich! And what do you think is going to happen as the developing countries of this world adopt North-American style eating habits? All this destruction is going to multiply, multiply, multiply!

Sam: Uhhh …

Sally: You're hopeless! It's hopeless! See you later!

Sam: I think I've lost my appetite.

Do you ever feel like Sally, or Sam? In your opinion, is Sally a complete alarmist, or does she make some good points? Do blissful ignorance and denial or paralyzing guilt and anxiety sometimes seem like the only possible reactions to such overwhelming problems? Point out that there is an alternative to both Sam's and Sally's attitudes. We can look for ways to support sustainable agriculture, and we can do so out of hope and joy.

8.
READINGS
"What is sustainable agriculture?" (p. 33)
"Three good reasons to support small local farmers" (p. 296)

What are examples of sustainable agriculture you've encountered? Do you know farmers who are actively improving their farm's soil, water quality, treatment of animals, biodiversity, or community involvement? Now may be a good time to explore the difference between sustainable agriculture and organic agriculture (as defined on page 336). The two often overlap but aren't necessarily synonymous. Supermarket food labeled "organic" may have been grown on a mass scale and shipped thousands of miles using fossil fuels.

It's also important to emphasize that most conventional farmers face enormous pressures, economic and otherwise, that make switching to alternative methods difficult. For decades, government subsidies, most university agriculture programs, and other aspects of the farm support infrastructure have been designed to promote large-scale, conventional methods. All farmers need a listening ear and compassion, not condemnation.

How does sustainable agriculture enhance human quality of life? In addition to securing natural resources for our future, sustainable agriculture helps us connect to those growing our food, building stronger community bonds and creating a better life for farmers. And the food is fresher and tastier. Close with a prayer of thanks for God's delicious blessings.

REVIEW SESSION 2
Creation

KEY IDEAS

• Environmental issues are not separate from overall human concerns. The health of the air, soil, water, and wildlife are directly related to our own health, and to that of our children and grandchildren.

• Modern agribusiness is focused on producing large quantities at low financial cost.

• "Sustainable agriculture" is focused on creating a system that can go on indefinitely. It must be economically viable, but it also must care for the land and provide a good quality of life for all concerned.

PRAYER

Think of the sounds (such as falling rain), smells (freshly-turned soil), and sights (bright green shoots) of creation that are part of the system for creating tastes (food). Compose a prayer of gratitude to God for these good gifts.

INVITATIONS TO ACTION

• Walk slowly and mindfully through a piece of land that's important to you (as described on page 67 of *Simply in Season*).

• Get local: Learn more about agriculture in your area—talk with a farmer if possible. What grain crops, fruits, vegetables, and animals are grown or raised? How large is the average farm?

• Explore the Invitations to Action in the Spring chapter (p. 80).

PREVIEW SESSION 3
Health

Skim the *Simply in Season* Summer chapter, which focuses on health.

Reflect on this scripture: "The earth brought forth vegetation ... trees of every kind bearing fruit with the seed in it. And God saw that it was good" (Genesis 1:12). How have you experienced God's good gift of food? Has overexposure to cheap, nonnutritious food affected you physically, emotionally, spiritually?

For the next core session, bring an item or two of store-purchased food from your pantry, such as bread, canned soup, soda, or condiments.

SESSION 3
Health

KEY IDEAS

- As rates of obesity and related diseases rise, North America's cheap, abundant food supply has become both a blessing and a curse.

- God calls us to consider what is "enough" and to treat our bodies with respect.

- Depending on how food is grown/raised, it can either damage or build up the health of the people and communities doing the growing.

MATERIALS NEEDED

- Supermarket items brought in by participants (for Corn Syrup Cornucopia activity)

- Copies of Review/Preview handout found at end of this session (Printer-friendly versions are available to download online at simplyinseason.org.)

BIBLE REFLECTION

"The earth brought forth vegetation ... trees of every kind bearing fruit with the seed in it. And God saw that it was good." (Genesis 1:12)

In the creation story, God declares the plants and trees to be good and gives them to the first humans to eat (Genesis 1:29). From the beginning, food is linked with God's blessing. But food is also soon linked with human mortality. After disobeying God, Adam and Eve are dismissed from their garden paradise with the warning that obtaining food will now demand hard work, and that ultimately no food can save humans from death (Genesis 3:17-19).

For the rest of the Bible, humans' complex relationship with food is evident. Most people, like much of the world today, engaged in back-breaking labor to get enough calories and had few choices about what they would eat. But gluttony was also enough of a problem to cause some writers to caution against it (see Proverbs 23:21, for example). Today, we have the added complication of access to cheap, high-calorie but low-nutrient processed food, which makes obesity a disease of poverty as well as of wealth.

Those first stories in Genesis point toward a godly path to health. When we recognize food as God's gift, we are more likely to choose food that reflects God's desire for us to have healthy bodies and healthy communities. When we are aware of the work that went into our food, we are more likely to treat it and the people who grew it with respect.

1.

REVIEW: Allow time to share participants' prayers and responses to invitations to action. Continue your process of sharing ideas and local resources.

2.

READING

"Globesity: Too much, too little" (p. 128)

North American churches often pray for those around the world who don't have enough food—but rarely do we pray for those who have too much. **Has overexposure to cheap, nonnutritious food affected you physically, emotionally, or spiritually?**

3.

READINGS

"Ten nutrition tips" (p. 111)

"Healthy food and children" (p. 110)

These are long passages; choose a few sections to focus on, or give a summary. **How do you encourage healthy eating in your family? How do television, peer pressure, and other outside influences play into your family's eating choices?**

4.

ACTIVITY: CORN SYRUP CORNUCOPIA

Ask participants to bring in one or two store-bought, processed items from their pantry or refrigerator. These could include soda, canned soups, cereal, bread, condiments (ketchup, barbecue sauce, salad dressing). Be sure to include some "diet" products (lite salad dressing, etc.). Place the items on a table and ask the group to guess what they have in common. Inevitably, nearly all the items will contain corn syrup and/or high fructose corn syrup.

5.

READING

"Weighing the effects of corn syrup" (p. 149)

Corn syrup's ubiquity in U.S. products is largely due to federal commodity subsidies that result in a glut of cheap field corn. Much of the field corn processed in the United States is used for sweeteners. This is not a wise use of land, and it's not good for our bodies. **What are the alternatives?** Homemade versions of soup, scalloped potatoes, etc., usually don't include sweeteners at all. Check out sources of locally produced honey for desserts.

6.

How is choosing locally grown food from sustainable sources tied to a healthier lifestyle? Pages 120 and 147 note the health benefits to alternatives to typical supermarket eggs and meat. Fresh fruits and vegetables also contain more nutrients than those that have been shipped long distances and stored. Of course, gardening provides excellent exercise as well as nutrition. Encourage participants to also explore the idea of eating mindfully—savoring every spoonful and knowing the story behind the food.

7.

What could churches be doing to encourage healthy eating among members and in the larger community? Brainstorm ideas—for example, potlucks based on healthy, seasonal foods; sponsoring church/community gardens; preparing fresh, local food at a local soup kitchen. You may wish to refer to the following stories from the cookbook: Feeding the hungry fresh veggies (p. 241); Farmers working together so all can afford good food (p. 274).

8.

READINGS

"A miraculous wonder" (p. 106)

"Gardens for better health and stronger communities" (p. 143)

What are some of your own experiences with gardening? How is gardening connected to healthy, mindful eating?

9.

READINGS

(If your group will be doing the optional session on farmworkers, you may wish to omit the following questions.)

"At risk: farmworkers and their kids" (p. 124)

"Saving our bacon" (p. 115)

Our food choices affect not only our own health but also the health of our communities and the people who grow our food. Are you aware of the health issues of farmers and farmworkers in your area?

REVIEW SESSION 3
Health

KEY IDEAS

• As rates of obesity and related diseases rise, North America's cheap, abundant food supply has become both a blessing and a curse.

• God calls us to consider what is "enough" and to treat our bodies with respect.

• Depending on how food is grown/raised, it can either damage or build up the health of the people and communities doing the growing.

PRAYER

Pour out your feelings to God about your own health. This may take the form of a lament, or it may be a prayer of thanksgiving. Ask for God's guidance as you seek greater physical, emotional, and spiritual health.

INVITATIONS TO ACTION

• Brainstorm ideas for healthy eating from your own experiences. Are there particular recipes, approaches to meals, etc., that have been helpful in your family?

• Grow something! Whether it's herbs in a pot on a windowsill or rows and rows of neat vegetables, celebrate the joy of gardening.

• Get local: Look into local opportunities for enhancing community health, such as community or school gardens or nutrition teaching programs. Learn what health issues face local farmers and farmworkers.

• Explore an Invitation to Action from the Summer chapter of the cookbook (p. 174).

PREVIEW SESSION 4
Time

Skim the *Simply in Season* Autumn chapter, which focuses on time.

Reflect on this scripture: "For everything there is a season … a time to plant, and a time to pluck up that which is planted" (Ecclesiastes 3:1a, 2b). Does what you eat change with the seasons?

SESSION 4
Time

KEY IDEAS

· Eating locally means eating with the rhythm of the seasons.

· "Slow food" helps us savor God's gifts of nourishment. And it just tastes good!

· Finding creative ways to eat together and share food strengthens community bonds and adds joy to our lives.

MATERIALS NEEDED

- Large posterboards labeled with seasons or months of the year, seed catalogs or food magazines, scissors, glue (for What's in Season? activity)

- Several varieties of one type of fruit or vegetable (for Savoring Flavors activity)

- Copies of Review/Preview handout found at end of this session (Printer-friendly versions are available to download online at simplyinseason.org.)

BIBLE REFLECTION

"For everything there is a season ... a time to plant, and a time to pluck up that which is planted." (Ecclesiastes 3:1a, 2b)

Most of the biblical writers lived with an everyday awareness of the rhythms of agriculture: when various crops are sown and reaped, weather patterns, the life cycle of livestock. To the writer of Ecclesiastes, seedtime and harvest are as much a part of human life as birth and death. He and others associate God's presence not with a perpetual abundance of all crops, but rather with divinely appointed seasonal rhythms. After the flood, God assured Noah that "seedtime and harvest, cold and heat, summer and winter ... shall not cease" (Genesis 8:22). Seasonal changes were also part of the peace God promised to the faithful in Leviticus 26:3-5: "I will give you your rains in their season"; crops would be plentiful in their proper order, with grapes following grain.

What messages about fluctuations in abundance do we get from our current culture? Because our supermarkets carry items from all over the world, many of us have lost our connection to what's in season locally. On a larger scale, it's hard not to internalize the consumerism mindset that all pleasures—from fresh strawberries to stress-free relationships—should be available every hour of every day, every day of the year. Reclaiming a respect for the rhythms of life opens us up to different kinds of joy, from truly ripe, just-picked berries to relationships that endure in hard times. But most important, this reclamation makes available the deep peace that comes from recognizing God's presence in all times and seasons of life.

1.

REVIEW: Allow time to share participants' prayers and responses to Invitations to Action. Continue your process of sharing ideas—such as healthy eating ideas suggested in the last session—and local resources.

2.

READINGS

"Savoring the tastes of each season" (p. 182)

"A ritual of fall: cider-making" (p. 214)

Do you or your family have any eating rituals that are linked to the seasons (not just to particular holidays)? How about weekly rituals?

3.

ACTIVITY: WHAT'S IN SEASON?

This activity is designed to help participants examine their own understanding of when certain foods are in season locally. Again, tailor this activity to your own situation and participants' level of knowledge. To help make the point that food issues are something we're all still learning about, be sure to include some common examples and some obscure ones, both local and exotic.

Call out the names of fruits and vegetables and ask participants to say when they're available in your community or state. Write the names of the fruits and vegetables on a piece of paper labeled with the seasons or months of the year. Also include a category for produce that is never grown locally (bananas, for example). You may want to note how the use of local greenhouses affect/extend an item's availability.

Or, bring in seed catalogs and food magazines. Ask participants to cut out pictures of fruits and vegetables and paste them on a posterboard under the appropriate season or month. The cookbook could be used as a reference.

4.

READING

"Entitled to lettuce?" (p. 196)

Do you feel "entitled to lettuce"? What are some of the sacrifices involved in eating only locally grown produce? What are some of the joys? Encourage participants to explore the idea that sacrifices and joys are actually two sides of the same coin—in other words, "sacrificing," say, fresh berries in the winter enhances our joy when we taste them in all their freshness during the spring/summer.

5.

READING

"Slow food in a fast food culture" (p. 193)

"Sabbath for field and farmer" (p. 195)

Many modern agribusiness methods do not embrace the concept of the Sabbath—milk cows are not allowed to dry up, chickens are kept in perpetual light so as to lay more eggs, soil is pumped full of fertilizer rather than allowing it to rest. Farmers face huge pressures to maximize output, even if they would prefer to use other methods. **How do these attitudes reflect our culture as a whole? How do you observe the Sabbath?**

6.

ACTIVITY: Savoring flavors

With the rise of agribusiness and a culture focused on convenience, diversity in fruits, vegetables, and grains has suffered. Supermarket produce is usually bred for hardiness in shipping, rather than taste, and is dominated by a few varieties (for example, Big Boy tomatoes, Red Delicious apples, and iceberg lettuce). Leaders, visit a local farmers' market or orchard to obtain a diverse selection of one type of fruit or vegetable. Pass small chunks around for participants to savor.

7.

If we embrace the idea of "slow food," how can we make sure that preparing it doesn't become a burden? The first processed foods were often embraced by women tired of doing all the work of gardening, cooking, and cleaning up. It's important to acknowledge that wanting to cut down on time in the kitchen is not always a negative thing. Encourage participants to share ideas for creative time-saving as part of the Invitations to Actions.

8.

READINGS

"Dinner on a theme" (p. 197)

"Bringing together waste and need" (p. 185)

How have you creatively shared food with others? Have you ever been a part of a supper club or co-op? How about a community gardening project? Talk about your experiences.

REVIEW SESSION 4
Time

KEY IDEAS

• Eating locally means eating with the rhythm of the seasons.

• "Slow food" helps us savor God's gifts of nourishment. And it just tastes good!

• Finding creative ways to eat together and share food strengthens community bonds and adds joy to our lives.

PRAYER

Thank God for the blessings of each season. Focus on the sights, smells, sounds, and tastes of just one season, or write about all four.

INVITATIONS TO ACTION

• Make a slow meal: soak beans, simmer soup, knead bread. Invite friends to share it— or make the meal potluck.

• Make a list to share of creative ways you cut down on time cooking without using processed/convenience foods.

• Get local: Are there resources in your area for those who want to learn how to preserve food? Extension offices, community-supported agriculture farms, food co-ops and others often offer seminars in canning, drying, freezing, etc.

• Explore the Invitations to Action (p. 228) from the Autumn chapter of the cookbook.

PREVIEW SESSION 5
Money

Skim the *Simply in Season* Winter chapter, which focuses on money.

Reflect on this scripture: "The field of the poor may yield much food, but it is swept away through injustice" (Proverbs 13:23). How do you currently try to create a more just and merciful world through the use of your money?

SESSION 5
Money

KEY IDEAS

Searching out the lowest-priced food is not always the best way to be good stewards of our money.

Often it's the farmer, farmworker, and farming community paying the price for the low cost.

Buying local, seasonal foods (and fairly traded foods from far away when appropriate) benefits the farmer directly.

MATERIALS NEEDED

- An apple and a loaf of bread from the supermarket, a cup of coffee from a major coffee chain, and a knife for cutting the bread and apple (for Where Does the Money Go? activity)

- Copies of Review/Preview handout found at end of this session (Printer-friendly versions are available to download online at simplyinseason.org.)

BIBLE REFLECTION

"The field of the poor may yield much food, but it is swept away through injustice." (Proverbs 13:23)

The book of Proverbs warns repeatedly that laziness will lead to poverty and hunger. At the same time, the writer acknowledges in this saying and others that poverty can also stem from oppression—and he has harsh words for those who have power and treat the poor unfairly. Rulers who exploit poor people are like a hard rain, he says, which destroys rather than nurtures crops (28:3).

Those of us who have choices in what we eat are among the planet's powerful. Eating a variety of foods, eating meat more than a few times a year, purchasing nonessential items such as sugar, eating meals in restaurants—these are all hallmarks of wealth in many parts of the world. In our North American societies, on the other hand, poverty is often marked by limited opportunities to buy fresh fruits and vegetables and other nutritious foods. With power comes the responsibility—and opportunity—to learn the stories behind our food and the people who grow it, and to examine whether our food choices contribute to a just society. Our resources can then become nourishing rain to the gifts and potential of others.

1.

REVIEW: Allow time to share participants' prayers and responses to invitations to action. Continue your process of sharing ideas—such as the ideas for creative time-savers suggested in the last session—and local resources.

2.

When you do your regular grocery shopping, what role does price play in your decisions? Do you clip coupons, shop at discount stores, buy generic brands? Use the opening question to establish that we all want to be wise stewards of our money and that there are various ways to do so.

3.

On a larger scale, how do we use our money to create a world that reflects God's love for all? (i.e., tithe, give to charity, boycott particular products)

4.

READINGS
"The rise of agribusiness" (p. 292)
"Providing our food and living in poverty" (p. 258)

5.

ACTIVITY: WHERE DOES THE MONEY GO?
Have on display a cup of coffee from a major coffee chain, an apple, and a supermarket loaf of bread. Ask participants what percentage of these items' cost goes to the farmer (assuming that the apples and wheat for the bread are grown in the United States and the coffee is grown overseas).

To help participants visualize the answers, divide the foods to represent percentages:

- Cut the apple into five pieces and hold one up; the farmer receives 20 percent of the cost.

- Cut the bread into twenty pieces and hold one up; the farmer receives 5 percent of the cost.

- Pour out all but a tiny portion of the coffee; the farmer receives 1-2 percent.

Discuss why these percentages are so low. Of course, some of the costs of any food item must go to labor, transportation, storage, and processing (in the case of bread). But a huge percentage now also goes into marketing and corporate profits. And of course for more highly processed items, such as canned soup or frozen apple pie, the farmers' share would be even smaller.

Discuss alternatives, such as buying locally and forgoing highly processed items. **Are apples available locally in your area? How about grain/flour/bread? What about items that can't be grown locally in temperate climates, such as coffee?** If you plan to use the optional session on Fair Trade, simply introduce the concept. If not, you may want to take a bit more time to explain what fair trade is and where fair trade items are available locally (see Session E for resources).

(Sources: www.txbf.org; International Coffee Organization. Prices are in U.S. dollars.)

6.
What responsibility as Christians do we have to those who grow our food? The idea that cheapest is best is ingrained in many of us, but is that really the case?

7.
READING
"No lack of choice" (p. 256)
Using our money to buy fresh, local food—which may or may not cost more than the supermarket equivalent—is an exciting way to put our values into practice. Even the smallest step in that direction makes a difference. **Thinking about buying local food in this way, how might the two questions that led off this discussion be connected? In what ways is it good stewardship to buy local, seasonal food even if it costs more than other options?**

8.
READING
"Why poor people are getting heavier" (p. 129)
In North America, ironically, obesity strikes the poor especially hard *(see www.hungeractionnys.org/ObPovCSAs.pdf for a summary of the research on this issue)*. In addition to personal habits, societal factors behind this phenomenon include the lower cost of energy-dense food, lack of fresh produce in inner city stores, and fewer safe places to exercise. **What role can the church play in seeing that access to fresh, local food is not limited to the middle class and wealthy?**

9.

ACTIVITY: HIDDEN COSTS, HIDDEN WEALTH

Much of this study guide has focused on identifying the hidden costs of conventionally grown food—for example, healthcare costs related to obesity, loss of oil reserves, higher taxes to clean up environmental problems. As a group or individually, list all the costs of our food not reflected in the supermarket price but paid for in other ways. Then allow time for participants to reflect (using a journaling format, if desired) on another question: **We've learned about various types of costs. Now what are various types of wealth? What kinds of wealth would we like to experience in the future, and how might that wealth be related to our food choices?** Answers might include the wealth of strong relationships, the wealth of a clear conscience, or the wealth of time to cook good food and share it with others.

10.

CLOSING: Discuss plans for your final celebration and meal and pass out the "Next Steps" handout. Close with prayer, asking God for the wisdom to uncover hidden costs and thanking God for the opportunity to celebrate hidden wealth.

REVIEW SESSION 5
Money

KEY IDEAS

• Searching out the lowest-priced food is not always the best way to be good stewards of our money.

• Often it's the farmer, farmworker, and farming community paying the price for the low cost.

• Buying local, seasonal foods (and fairly traded foods from far away when appropriate) benefits the farmer directly.

PRAYER

Compose a prayer thanking God for the financial resources you have been given. Ask for God's guidance in using these resources and dealing with challenging questions of justice and charity.

INVITATIONS TO ACTION

• Evaluate your food budget. Are there processed items or restaurant meals you can give up so more money is available for fresh, local products or fair trade items? Or would you consider increasing your food budget itself for this purpose?

• Encourage your church to buy fair trade coffee, perhaps through the MCC Coffee Project (see mcc.org/us/washington/coffee).

• Get local: If you know a local farmer well enough to discuss financial issues, ask if it is getting harder or easier for them to meet financial goals. How else do they measure "success"?

• Explore the Invitations to Action (p. 278) from the Winter chapter of the cookbook.

PREVIEW SESSION 6
Celebration

The final session is a celebration of local food and stories. As you prepare a dish to share, reflect on what you've learned and experienced in this journey toward joy-filled eating. Look over the list of possible next steps and pray for guidance on what you'll choose to commit to.

Next steps

Here are ideas for the next steps you may take in your journey toward joy-filled eating. The ideas range from basic to radical. You may do some of them already. Put a check by anything new to which you'd like to commit. Keep this list and refer to it when you feel God may be nudging you to a new step on your food journey.

○ I will check labels in the supermarket produce section and choose items grown closest to my home.

○ I will visit a farmers' market and buy at least one locally grown item.

○ I will frequent farmers' markets and farm stands.

○ I will buy all my produce locally this summer and fall.

○ I will eliminate tropical fruits from my diet.

○ I will cook at least one seasonal meal per season.

○ I will cook at least one seasonal meal per week.

○ I will join a Community-Supported Agriculture farm.

○ I will express my appreciation to a seller at a farmers' market.

○ I will learn how and where the meat, eggs, and dairy products I consume are produced.

○ I will seek out local sources of meat, eggs, and dairy products.

○ I will buy only local meat, eggs, and dairy products.

○ I will get to know a local farmer or farmworker and ask questions about their work.

○ I will advocate for government policies that promote fair prices for farmers, both in North America and overseas.

○ I will prayerfully evaluate my household budget and consider how it can best reflect my values.

○ I will seek out fair trade sources of coffee, tea, chocolate, and other items.

○ I will buy only fair trade coffee, tea, or chocolate.

○ I will encourage my church or business to use only fair trade items during coffee hours.

○ I will eliminate as much as possible from my diet processed items that contain corn syrup.

○ I will reduce my use of convenience foods and increase use of whole foods.

○ I will find a local honey source and seek out recipes made with honey.

○ I will seek out local sources of grain products such as flour.

○ I will start one new seasonally based food ritual, such as making cider in autumn or celebrating the first strawberries of spring.

○ I will invite friends to a meal at least once a month.

○ I will notice and savor the smells and sounds of cooking as I work.

○ I will learn how to preserve a food item and do so.

○ I will offer up my health to God and seek God's guidance on maintaining it.

○ I will try beginning a meal with a prayer of thanksgiving.

○ I will begin all my meals with a prayer of thanksgiving.

○ I will pray once for the people who grow my food.

○ I will pray regularly for the people who grow my food.

○ I will plant a garden.

○ I will start a compost pile or bin.

○ I will grow herbs on my windowsill.

○ I will share what I've grown with others.

○ I will offer my expertise in gardening, canning, cooking to others in my church or community.

○ I will get involved with a local community gardening project.

SESSION 6
Celebration

• •

CELEBRATE: Enjoy a feast of local, seasonal foods and the stories behind them. Ask each participant to bring a dish to share. If the recipe doesn't come from *Simply in Season*, bring the recipe as well. If you like, list the local ingredients beside each dish. Provide a time for participants to share any stories behind where they found or grew the ingredients, or stories behind the recipe. You may want to introduce this time by reading some stories from the cookbook:

READINGS
"All we have hoped for" (p. 331)
"A crop of healthy children" (p. 166)
"Cherish that sweet potato" (p. 238)

You may also ask participants to share how they plan to celebrate hope in their own eating choices. What are their "sweet potatoes," their tangible connection to a vision of a hope-filled food future? Invite participants who feel comfortable to share which "Next Steps" they've committed to. You may want to have a brief ceremony in which all participants jot their commitments on a piece of paper and place them in a basket. If you are compiling a booklet of participants' prayers, ideas, and local resources, distribute this now. End with prayer.

OPTIONAL SESSIONS

The following sessions are designed to complement and expand upon certain themes in the core sessions. The first four optional sessions are tied to specific core sessions; we suggest you use them after the session listed in parentheses. The other three optional sessions could be used at any time but may be most helpful near the end of your study. These sessions are intended to help your group dig more deeply into particular topics that are of interest to them and to connect with local resources. They are structured a bit more loosely than the core sessions; feel free to adapt them to your group's interests and experience.

Animals Session

(Use after Session 2: Creation)

DESCRIPTION

Learn more about the stories behind our meat, milk, and eggs. Open with a quick introduction to confinement operations and why they exist. Then summarize the health benefits of products from animals raised with access to sunshine, exercise, and the diet for which they are best suited. Choose from several options for learning more. Discuss how you currently make decisions about which meat, eggs, and milk products to buy, and explore options for buying products from animals raised locally and sustainably.

PREPARATION NEEDED

- Make a recipe with local meat, milk, or eggs for this session's snack.

- Bring in an egg from the supermarket and one from a local free-range hen to compare.

- If you like, create an overhead transparency of the Concentrated Animal Feeding Operations (CAFO) quiz.

- Choose a Learning Option and prepare accordingly, whether by assigning topics to research and distributing the resource list or inviting speakers.

- Research local sources of products from animals raised sustainably.

OPENING

Begin by cracking open two eggs—one a typical supermarket egg, and one from a local free-range hen. Explain that the darker orange of the latter egg's yolk reflects extra beta-carotene, while it also has 10 percent less fat, 40 percent more vitamin A, and 400 times more healthful omega-3 fatty acids. Similarly, other animals fed the diet to which their bodies were designed (grass, in the case of cows), produce more healthful meat and milk.

So why don't all our meat, milk, and eggs come from animals given access to sunlight, movement, and the diet to which they are best suited? Read "CAFOs 101" (p. 300) for an overview of "concentrated animal feeding operations." Confined animals can be fed grain, given growth hormones, and subjected to other practices that bring them to market weight more quickly, or produce the maximum amount of milk and eggs—which lowers the cost for the customer.

You may wish to use the CAFO Quiz to prompt further discussion or reflection. If you choose the first learning option, it may be most effective to have participants take the quiz before the presentations on how animals are raised but not go over the answers until the end of the class; most of the questions should be answered through the presentations. The correct answers are: 1. C; 2. D; 3. B; 4. D; 5. A. *(Sources: www.factoryfarm.org, www.gracelinks.org)*

LEARNING OPTION 1

If your group is interested in learning more about the details of how most animals are raised in North America, distribute copies of the resource list and have them divide into small groups or pairs to research a particular animal product (beef, pork, chicken, fish/seafood, eggs, and milk are those most likely to be raised in large operations). Each team should prepare a five-minute presentation that answers some of the following questions (examples are given using pork as the food being researched):

- What percentage of commercially available pork comes from confinement operations?

- What's the typical life cycle for a hog at such an operation?

- What are the living conditions? What are the animals fed? How much space do they have to move around? Are they given antibiotics or growth hormones? How often do they give birth? What happens to sick hogs? How are animals slaughtered? (If there's time, the team may wish to compare these conditions to hogs raised on small farms that focus on sustainable practices.)

- What other practices are used to maximize output?

- What environmental issues do large-scale hog operations face?

LEARNING OPTION 2

Invite one or more local animal farmers to share about their work and experience. Ideally, these would be people with experience with both conventional and sustainable agriculture who would be able to compare their experiences. Ask each farmer to describe their operation—how many animals, how they are housed and fed, daily routines, where they market their products. Are they available locally? How does their operation compare to others for the same product? How have their practices changed over time, or from the previous generation, and why? How is their health affected by their work? Do they feel that it is meaningful work? What role do they see themselves playing in the local community? What environmental factors do they take into consideration? What motivates them to follow the methods they do? What do they wish people understood about this kind of work?

LEARNING OPTION 3

For groups already familiar with animal-raising practices, arrange for several people (regular participants or others you've invited) to share how they make decisions about buying or raising animal products. This could include someone who is committed to buying only products from animals raised in a humane, environmentally responsible manner; someone who buys typical products from the supermarket but eats meat only occasionally; a complete vegetarian; and someone who raises their own animals for meat, eggs, or milk (or, in the case of meat, someone who hunts their own meat). Ask them how they came to their decisions, whether any personal sacrifices have been required, and how they've benefited from their decisions. You may wish to solicit other questions from the group ahead of time.

DISCUSSION QUESTIONS

• How do you make your decisions about whether or where to buy animal products?

• How does your faith come into play?

• Do you know the stories behind the meat, milk, or eggs you buy?

• Have you ever raised an animal for food?

• Do we as Christians have an obligation to treat animals with mercy?

LOCAL RESOURCES

Provide participants with a list of places to buy local meat, milk, and eggs from animals raised sustainably. If you have difficulty, see the list of Web sites under "Finding local food" in the resources section.

ANIMAL RESOURCES

- Categorized by animal:
  www.factoryfarm.org
  www.ers.usda.gov/Briefing
  www.farmsanctuary.org

- Beef: www.mercola.com/2002/apr/17/cattle1.htm — Article from the *New York Times* (March 31, 2002) that traces the life of a conventionally raised steer.

- Pork: Scully, Matthew. *Dominion: the Power of Man, the Suffering of Animals, and the Call to Mercy* (book). New York: St. Martin's Press, 2002. Chapter titled "Deliver me from my necessities" focuses on how hogs are raised.

- Fish/seafood: www.grist.org/advice/books/2000/02/09/a/ — Excerpt from *Salmon Nation: People and Fish on the Edge* that focuses on salmon fishing.

- Eggs: www.chickenout.ca — Anti-battery cage campaign from the Vancouver Humane Society.

CAFO QUIZ
(Concentrated Animal Feeding Operation)

1. In the United States, what percentage of poultry sold in super-markets is produced by corporations, as opposed to family farms?
○ 50 percent
○ 75 percent
○ 98 percent

2. Which of the following are sows (mother hogs) in typical confinement operations able to do:
○ Turn around in their cages.
○ Root through straw or dirt, as is their natural instinct.
○ Go longer than one week without being pregnant or nursing.
○ None of the above.

3. In a conventional feedlot system, how much grain and how many quarts of gasoline (used to grow the grain) are needed to produce one pound of beef?
○ 1 lb. of grain, and one quart of gasoline
○ 5 lbs. of grain, and one quart of gasoline
○ 3 lbs. of grain, and two quarts of gasoline

4. Which of the following is NOT used to maximize production on large-scale confinement farms?
○ Dairy cows are reimpregnated while they are still lactating from their previous birth.
○ Broiler (meat) chickens have been bred to grow twice as large, twice as fast, which puts tremendous strain on their legs, heart, and lungs.
○ Layers (egg) chickens undergo "force molting," in which they are deprived of food and water for days in order to shock their bodies into another laying cycle.
○ Fish are forced to listen to bad disco music until they agree to spawn.

5. According to a study by leading real estate appraisal analysts, property located next to a CAFO decreases in value by how much (due to perceived and actual environmental impact of CAFOs)?
○ 50 to 90 percent
○ 30 to 60 percent
○ 10 to 40 percent

Farmworkers Session

(Use after Session 3: Health)

DESCRIPTION

Learn about the conditions facing those who harvest much of the food grown in the United States and Canada, and discuss our responsibility to our "invisible neighbors."

PREPARATION NEEDED

- Snack suggestions: chips and salsa (such as Fresh Summer Salsa, p. 163), or another treat celebrating fresh produce and Latinos' culinary heritage.

- Select a video/DVD option and preview it.

- Learn about farmworkers in your own community, if applicable.

OPENING

Remind participants of the food production chain activity from the very first lesson. Did your chain include the worker who picked the supermarket tomato? Seasonal farm workers (some of whom are migrants, and some of whom live in one place year-round) face some of the poorest working conditions and lowest wages of any group in the United States and Canada. Many laws designed to protect laborers do not apply to farm workers.

READINGS

"Our invisible neighbors" (p. 302)
"Providing our food and living in poverty" (p. 258)
"At risk: farmworkers and their kids" (p. 124)

Note that most farmworkers are immigrants, and many are undocumented, which leaves them especially vulnerable to mistreatment and unfair labor practices.

VIDEO OPTION 1

Watch "Justice on the Table," a 25-minute video released in 2003 and funded by the National Presbyterian Hunger Program (available for $20 from www.moving-image.com). According to the film's producers, "'Justice on the Table' listens to farmworkers themselves tell of their treatment in Oregon's fields, and highlights their contributions to our regional and national economic prosperity." Includes a study guide with facts and discussion questions. This film issues a clear call for justice for immigrants and would be especially appropriate for groups interested in discussing how immigration issues play into our food supply.

VIDEO OPTION 2

Watch "The Battle Fields: The Coalition of Immokalee Workers vs. Taco Bell," a 15-minute recording of a PBS NOW news program segment originally aired in May 2005. (View online at www.pbs.org/now/society/ciw.html# or request a free DVD by e-mailing the coalition at workers@ciw-online.org.) This program tells the story of a coalition of Florida farmworkers' successful campaign to ensure a major corporation's cooperation in obtaining better working conditions and wages. This option focuses less on immigration issues and would be especially appropriate for groups interested in hearing about real-life advocacy stories.

DISCUSSION QUESTIONS

- Have you thought previously about the issues raised in this video/DVD? Have you had past experience with farmworkers and farmworkers' issues? (These answers may vary widely depending on your location and the type of crops grown nearby.)

- What are our responsibilities, as Christians, to farmworkers and others who are involved in the production of our food? (Note that other agriculture-related industries, such as meatpacking, also employ large numbers of easily exploited immigrants.)

- How does choosing locally grown food play into this responsibility? Generally, the closer we are to the source of our food the more easily we can find out the conditions under which it was harvested, and we can more easily advocate for change if necessary. If we do in fact buy all our produce from local, ethical sources, do we still have a responsibility to advocate for better conditions in the larger system? Or should our efforts be focused on creating a new kind of system? Or should we do both?

- The question of fair treatment of farmworkers raises broader questions about immigration policies, and the vast economic disparities between immigrants' home and host countries. How might policies that encourage access to local markets, both in the United States and in other countries, affect our current immigration situation?

BRAINSTORM

Create a list of positive steps your group can take to work toward better treatment of farmworkers in the United States and a more humane system of food production. These might include: learning more about farmworkers in your area, choosing foods grown under ethical conditions, joining the Immokalee coalition in its current campaign to seek cooperation from other fast food chains, advocating for national laws that would offer farmworkers more legal protections, and advocating for policies that would improve the economic situations of immigrants' home countries.

Bible and Food Session

(Use after Session 4: Time)

DESCRIPTION

Explore how the Bible depicts food, both eating and growing it. Identify themes that run throughout the Bible in relation to food, and then look closely at several stories that relate to ideas discussed in Session 4 (Time).

PREPARATION NEEDED

- Remind participants to bring their Bibles, ideally with a concordance, for this session.

- Because bread is mentioned so often in the Bible and has so many symbolic connotations, a bread recipe from *Simply in Season* would be an ideal snack for this session.

OPENING

Note that food is important in the Bible, both on a physical level and a symbolic level. Humans' separation from God began with the fruit eaten by Eve and Adam in the garden; our reconciliation through Jesus is symbolized by (or, in some Christian traditions, takes place through) the bread and wine of communion.

BIBLE BRAINSTORM

Ask participants to think of all the Bible stories/passages they know that relate to eating and growing food and list these on a large piece of paper. A concordance is a helpful tool here—look for passages containing the words food, eat, bread, fish, fruit, drink, plant, harvest, etc.

Then ask if any themes emerge. These might include generosity (injunctions to share with the poor, the boy who gave his food for the feeding of the five thousand); setting community boundaries (laws about clean and unclean food; conflict among the early Christians about doing away with these laws; Jesus causing scandals by eating with sinners); food as a gift from God (manna from heaven; the widow whose oil and flour were miraculously renewed; Jesus' calls not to worry about food) and hospitality (stories in which guests are welcomed with food or a drink). In addition, participants may note that food-related metaphors, especially related to harvest and planting, also play an important role in the Bible.

Ask participants: What strikes you about these themes? How do they relate to what you've discovered about joy-filled eating?

IN-DEPTH DISCUSSION

Break into pairs or small groups to read and discuss the following ideas and Bible passages. As time allows, have each group report on their discussion.

Feasting vs. everyday eating: John 2:1-11 (Jesus turns water into wine at the wedding at Cana); John 21:1-14 (Jesus prepares bread and fish for the disciples).

In many cultures, everyday food is simple and repetitive, with little meat or sweets. Weddings, funerals, and other events and holidays, however, are a time of relatively extravagant feasting. What does Jesus' first miracle tell us about his attitude toward celebrations/feasts? Is this different from your own attitude or the one with which you were raised? *(Note: This is not intended to be a discussion about whether Christians should drink alcohol.)* How has our culture blurred the line between feasting and everyday eating? How might we benefit if we recaptured the joy of saving certain foods for special occasions?

In the passage from John, the disciples' nets become miraculously full. They then share a simple meal of bread and fish already prepared by Jesus, whom they recognize as the risen Lord. Their ordinary meal has become a sacred experience. Read "Ordinary miracles" (p. 220). How can we learn not to take for granted God's gift of "ordinary" food and the creation that makes it possible? How can we make both our daily meals and our feasts a time of gratitude and recognizing God's presence?

Guidelines for eating: Leviticus 11 (Israelites' original dietary laws), Romans 14:14-21 (Paul urges early church not to let laws divide them).

What is your reaction when reading the dietary laws that God gave to the Israelites? What do you think their original purpose was? How might they have played a positive role in creating community boundaries, health, and drawing one nearer to God in everyday life? Why did the early Christians eventually do away with such laws?

We in the United States and Canada have no government-established dietary laws, but many of us have internalized the rules of good eating that advertisements would like us to believe; for example, the rule that faster is better. What other rules, explicit or implicit, guide our society's food choices? (These needn't all be negative. For example, the USDA Food Pyramid, the idea that "real" meals contain meat, the unacceptability of eating insects, or horse or dog meat.)

Is it possible for Christians to imagine new guidelines for eating that don't lend themselves to legalism or creating divisions? If you are from a Christian tradition that observes eating practices (such as abstaining from meat at certain times of the year), what role do these practices play in your spiritual life? Read "Imagining modern day dietary laws for right eating," p. 210. What values do these "laws" reflect? What would your own guidelines for eating with justice and joy look like?

The power of sharing food with others: Matthew 25:34-46 (Jesus' command to share with "the least of these"); 2 Samuel 9 (David).

This Matthew passage is a familiar one, but often the strength of Jesus' words is not acknowledged. What does he say will happen to those who do not share food with the hungry? Jesus says that sharing our food with "the least of these" is the same as sharing it with him. Have you experienced Jesus' presence in someone with whom you've eaten a meal? Have you been on the receiving end of a gift of food, whether from someone who was better or worse-off than you? How did it make you feel? What opportunities do you regularly have to share food (not just money for food, but food itself) with someone who is hungry? How about someone who may not be physically malnourished, but is spiritually or emotionally hungry?

The story of David and Mephibosheth is less well known. Note how many times the phrase "you will eat at my table" or something like it is used. What does that tell you about the importance in this culture of being invited to eat with someone? What meaning has sharing food had for you in the past? How has it strengthened your bonds with those with whom you've eaten? Have you ever refused to eat with someone, or had someone refused to eat with you?

In your congregation or group, when do you usually eat together, or invite others to eat with you? Are there ways you might expand these opportunities to share food, without placing an unacceptable burden on those who prepare the food?

Globalization Session

(Use after Session 4: Time)

DESCRIPTION

Examine the issue of economic globalization's impact on farmers by watching "A Plate Half Full" (MCC, 17 minutes). This video/DVD tells the stories of two farmers—one from the Philippines, one from Kansas. Discussion afterward can help participants connect how supporting local farmers is a concrete way to address problems that may seem overwhelmingly large and complex.

PREPARATION NEEDED

- Leaders may want to view the video/DVD in advance.

- Suggest Web sites with information on globalization for participants who would like to explore this topic before the class. (Or hand out the list afterward to everyone.) Or suggest that they read the cookbook writings indexed under "globalization."

OPENING

Ask participants what they think of when they hear the words "economic globalization" as it applies to food. They may list things such as trade laws, subsidies, and imports/exports; mention greater access to tropical fruits; or describe feeling overwhelmed by the seeming complexity or this topic. Emphasize that amid all the statistics and controversy it's important to listen to the stories of individuals affected by globalization. View "A Plate Half Full."

DISCUSSION QUESTIONS

- "Our food security is responsible for someone else's insecurity" (line from the video): Is this an accurate description of our current situation? Do we, in fact, have a responsibility to the people who grow the world's food supply?

- This video demonstrates the element of uncertainty (of the weather, markets, etc.) that has always existed in agriculture. Do we run the risk of romanticizing farming? How can we help farmers around the world obtain more security? How does eating local, seasonal food contribute to this goal?

- The farmer from Kansas would like his son to farm. He says, "We'll just keep planting our crops" and hoping for the best. Do small farmers have other options for making sure that their farming is sustainable and their children have a chance to carry it on? Are farmers in your area facing these issues? How are they dealing with them? How can Christian congregations and communities make a difference?

Fair Trade Session

(Use after Session 5: Money)

DESCRIPTION

Learn about fair trade—what it is, how it benefits farmers around the world, and where fair trade food and beverages can be purchased locally. Discuss how fair trade items fit into an overall ethic of basing one's diet on local, seasonal food.

PREPARATION NEEDED

- For this session's snack, bring in fair trade treats. Try Hazelnut Coffee Brownies (p. 270) made with fair trade coffee and chocolate, along with a selection of coffee, tea, and cocoa. You may find other items, from bananas to olive oil, available in your area or online. You may also want to bring in a fair trade item to serve as a prize for the quiz winner.

- If you are not familiar with the concept of fair trade, read the definition on page 336 of the cookbook. Several Web sites listed in the Resources section offer information and resources on fair trade in general and coffee specifically.

- Research where fair trade food can be purchased locally. The Ten Thousand Villages site, www.tenthousandvillages.com, includes store location and product information for the United States and Canada. You can also check your local supermarkets, food co-ops, etc., to see if they carry any fair trade items.

- Prepare for the activity described below.

- Explore options for serving fair trade coffee at your church. The MCC U.S. Coffee Project invites Mennonite and Brethren in Christ congregations to serve fair trade coffee and other beverages. You can download a brochure at www.mcc.org/us/washington/coffee. The Coffee Project is a collaboration with Equal Exchange, a fair trade company. For other denominational groups working with Equal Exchange, go to www.equalexchange.com/interfaith-program.

- You may want to invite someone from a nearby church that serves fair trade coffee to share that congregation's experiences.

OPENING

Remind participants of the "Where does the money go?" activity from Session 5. Of all the farmers, the coffee farmers received the lowest share of profit from their work. Farmers and farmworkers in poor countries, where most coffee-growing regions are located, are even more vulnerable to market fluctuations and dishonest middlemen than farmers in the United States and Canada.

ACTIVITY

An excellent tool to help participants visualize where their money actually goes when they buy coffee can be found at www.pbs.org/frontlineworld/stories/guatemala.mexico/coffee1.html. This interactive feature allows participants to decide how they would allocate their coffee dollar among growers, traders, shippers, roasters, and retailers. It then gives the real-world breakdown and explains each part of the coffee trading process. If possible, set up a computer with a projected screen and walk through the tool together. If this isn't possible, use the information for your own "coffee dollar" activity. Bring in 20 nickels and ask participants to allocate them among the five groups. Then discuss what each group actually receives and why. *(Note: The percentage of profit received by the farmer is higher in this activity than in the previous one. That's because the "Where does the money go?" activity refers specifically to a cup of coffee purchased from a coffee shop, while the activity in this session refers to all coffee.)*

DISCUSSION QUESTIONS

- So what's the alternative to this system? Explain the idea of fair trade (see the definition on page 336 of the cookbook). Inquire whether anyone currently buys fair trade items, and why. Look at the readings "Justice, java, and Hurricane Mitch" (p. 270) and "Spending the extra dime" (p. 239).

- In Session 5 (Money), the idea of putting one's values into practice by buying local food was discussed. What values might we put into practice by buying fair trade items?

- How does fair trade fit into an overall ethic of basing one's diet on local, seasonal food? Does the fair trade label automatically make something a wise purchase? How does fair trade offer us a chance to connect with brothers and sisters around the world?

- Explain the MCC U.S. Coffee Project (or your own denomination's fair trade coffee project) and its goal of encouraging congregations to serve fair trade beverages during coffee hours and other gatherings. Is this something in which your church or campus could participate?

SPECIAL GUEST

If you've invited guests from a congregation that serves and promotes fair trade products, ask them to share about their experiences: how they got interested in fair trade, the logistics of switching to fair trade beverages, the reception they've gotten from congregation members, and other activities they may be doing to learn about or promote fair trade items.

Local Farmers Session

DESCRIPTION

Hear the first-hand stories of people who grow and sell food in your area. Invite several local people involved in sustainable or conventional farming or food production to share about their work. This can be as formal or informal as you want to make it.

PREPARATION NEEDED

- Invite your guests—and ask them to bring samples if they like. Ideas for whom to invite: owner of a local CSA, vegetable/fruit farmer with a farm stand or farmers' market booth, conventional or organic crop (corn, wheat, soybeans, barley, oats) farmer, conventional or organic livestock farmer, someone who raises chickens or other animals as a hobby or side business, representative from a restaurant or store that sells local food, owners of a large fruit and vegetable farm, workers on a large fruit and vegetable farm, fertilizer/pesticide or farm equipment salesperson, someone who makes food products using local supplies (for example, a cheesemaker or baker), a bee-keeper.

- Ask participants to submit questions ahead of time. Include questions that allow the guests to share both the challenges and joys of their work, and how they see it connecting with their faith or values.

- Organize questions.

- Provide refreshments, if desired, for a time of informal chatting after the panel discussion.

SPECIAL GUESTS

Ask guests to introduce themselves and tell a bit about what they do. Ask questions submitted by participants. These may apply to all the speakers or just to one or two. Make sure everyone has a chance to talk. Allow for spontaneous question and answer session afterward; and, if time allows, an informal time of mingling over refreshments. If applicable, invite guests to provide you with a business card or other contact information to add to your list of local resources.

Advocacy Session

DESCRIPTION

Explore the concept of advocacy—speaking to government in an effort to shape policies—and how it relates to the ideal of healthful, joy-filled eating. You may want to tie this session into a particular local issue.

PREPARATION NEEDED

- For those in the United States, ask participants to read the MCC Washington Office Guide to Food and Farming (available in PDF format at http://www.mcc.org/us/washington/resources.html). You may print out copies of the guide for those without access to the Internet, or order print versions by calling the Washington Office at (202) 544-6564.

- If there are any current "hot" or ongoing issues in your area related to farming or eating—for example, a community group fighting a new mega-farm, or concerns over farmworkers' treatment—bring in background information (newspaper articles, etc.), and the names and contact information of relevant government officials.

- You may also want to have available the names and contact information of your state/provincial and national representatives.

OPENING

Begin by asking whether anyone in the class has ever been involved in advocacy at any level—meeting with a local official, writing a letter to one's representative at a national level, etc. What prompted that involvement?

DISCUSSION

Discuss the concept of advocacy in general. How does our faith influence how we speak to government? Most Mennonites for many years had a stance of noninvolvement in political affairs, including voting. For those from that faith tradition, how does that background affect your current views on advocacy?

Explore how speaking to government connects with a desire to make food choices that care for creation, our health, and the health of our communities. Do we have a responsibility to advocate for policies that will benefit both ourselves and our neighbors around the world—and the next generations? Participants' opinions may vary on this issue; try to make sure that all voices are respected.

If you have any current relevant local issues, share the background information and discuss these now. How might the values that drive our food choices affect how we respond to these issues?

Look at the section on page two of the Washington Office guide titled "Taking a Bite out of Injustice: Alternative Policies." Is there a particular issue or two on this list that you find especially compelling? Share ideas for further involvement.

Resources

GENERAL INFORMATION ON CORE THEMES
(see page 335 of "Simply in Season" cookbook for more)

www.gracelinks.org — From the Global Resource Action Center for the Environment. Includes an information-packed section called Sustainable Table. One feature is a list of terms and labels (such as organic, pasture-raised, hormone-free).

www.earthministry.org — Earth Ministry is a Christian creation care organization. Site includes a Food and Farming section with links and congregational resources.

Pollan, Michael. **The Omnivore's Dilemma: A Natural History of Four Meals** (book). Penguin Press HC, 2006. The author traces the origins of four meals from four food "chains" (industrial, "big organic," sustainable/local, and personal). Includes more information on nearly every theme discussed in the curriculum.

The Future of Food (video). 89 minutes. Lily films, www.thefutureof-food.com. Shot on location in the United States, Canada and Mexico, this film examines the complex web of market and political forces that are changing what we eat as corporations seek to control the world's food system, and presents ideas for alternatives.

SIMPLY IN SEASON AND MCC

www.simplyinseason.org — The official *Simply in Season* site. Includes the cookbook's entire fruit and vegetable guide.

http://simplyinseason.blogspot.com — News and reflections on all that's good about local food from the co-author of *Simply in Season*.

www.mcc.org — Mennonite Central Committee is the relief, development, and peacebuilding agency of U.S. and Canadian Mennonite and Brethren and Christ churches. Resources section includes books and videos/DVDs on food, development, and environmental issues.

FINDING LOCAL FOOD

www.nal.usda.gov/afsic/csa/ — Links to several Community Supported Agriculture searches (U.S. and Canada).

http://marketplace.chef2chef.net/farmer-markets/canada.htm — Find farmers' markets near you (Canada).

http://www.ams.usda.gov/farmersmarkets/ — Find farmers' markets near you (U.S.)

www.localharvest.org — Find farmers' markets, CSAs, farm stands, restaurants, and sources of specific products including meat and eggs in your area (U.S.)

www.eatwellguide.org — Find sources of sustainably raised animal products near you (U.S.)

ANIMALS

www.factoryfarm.org — News and information about confinement-based animal operations.

www.eatwild.com — Information about the benefits of raising animals on pasture. Includes links to producers.

Scully, Matthew. **Dominion: the Power of Man, the Suffering of Animals, and the Call to Mercy** (book). New York: St. Martin's Press, 2002. A conservative, Christian author examines animal welfare. Includes a chapter on confinement operations.

www.themeatrix.com — Fun animated spoofs of The Matrix movies, in which the heroes battle inhumane treatment of farm animals.

FARMWORKERS

www.ciw-online.org — The Coalition of Immokalee Workers has gained international attention for its successful campaign to obtain higher pay from Taco Bell for tomato pickers.

www.cmfn.org — The Catholic Migrant Farmworker Network is dedicated to pastoral ministry with farmworkers. Site includes recordings of personal stories from farmworkers.

www.ufw.org — Founded by Cesar Chavez, United Farm Workers is the major labor union through which farm workers in the United States organize for better conditions. Includes news, links, and resources.

GLOBALIZATION AND ADVOCACY/GOVERNMENT POLICIES

www.mcc.org/washington — The MCC U.S. Washington Office provides opportunities for advocacy on many issues. Resources address globalization and include an advocacy handbook to assist in witness to the government.

www.mcc.org/canada/ottawa/government/ — Tips on contacting Canadian government officials from the MCC Ottawa office.

www.iatp.org — The Institute for Agriculture and Trade Policy "promotes resilient family farms, rural communities and ecosystems around the world."

FAIR TRADE

www.tenthousandvillage.com — Ten Thousand Villages sells fair trade items from around the world, including coffee, tea, chocolate, and other food items. Site includes a store locator for the United States and Canada.

www.equalexchange.org — Equal Exchange is a fair trade company that partners with churches and denominations to promote and serve fair trade coffee.

www.levelground.org — Level Ground is a Canadian fair trade company that sells coffee, dried fruit, and other products.